18th Century Lovers

A BOOK OF DAYS

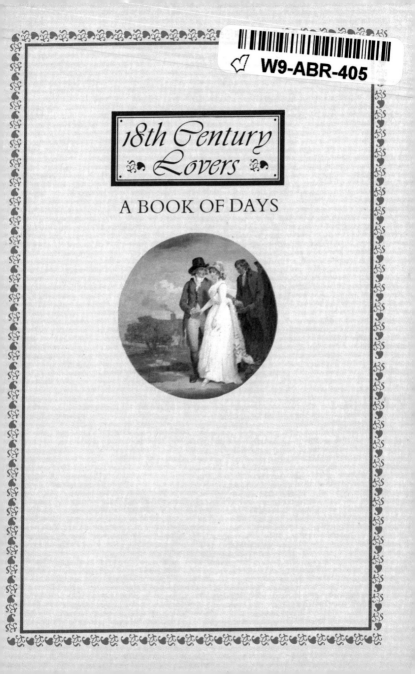

18th Century Lovers

A BOOK OF DAYS

The Conquest of Love is our destiny; we must
follow it.

Pierre Choderlos de Laclos 1741-1803
Les Liaisons Dangereuses

CENTURY BENHAM
London   Sydney   Auckland   Johannesburg

First published in Great Britain in 1990
by Century Benham Ltd
A division of Century Hutchinson Publishing Group
Brookmount House, 62-65 Chandos Place,
London WC2N 4NW

Copyright © Phoebe Phillips Editions 1990

Also available: *Medieval Lovers: A Book of Days*

Whilst every effort has been made to ensure
accuracy, the publishers cannot accept liability
for any errors.

Set in Bembo by Spectrum Typesetting Ltd

Printed and bound in Spain by
Gráficas Estella, S.A. Navarra.

Designed and produced by PHOEBE PHILLIPS EDITIONS

ISBN 0 7126 3561 0

Illustrations:
Front cover: *The Food of Love*
Back cover: *A Hand Held a Heart's Plea*
Half title: *Love and Charity*
Title: *Love Surprised – an eternal game of love*

Foreword

Love, and your fears will vanish. In place of the
things that terrify you, you will discover delicious
feelings, a tender and submissive lover, and all your
days, given over to happiness, will leave you with
no other regret than that you wasted so many of
them in indifference!

Pierre Choderlos de Laclos 1741-1803 · Les Liaisons Dangereuses

January

_____

1

_____

2

_____

3

_____

4

_____

5

_____

6

_____

7

_____

The Shyness of Love Encouraged by Music

Beneath the myrtle's secret shade,
  When Delia blessed my eyes;
At first I viewed the lovely maid
  In silent soft surprise.
With trembling voice, and anxious mind,
  I softly whispered love;
She blushed a smile so sweetly kind,
  Did all my fears remove.
Her lovely yielding form I pressed,
  Sweet maddening kisses stole;
And soon her swimming eyes confessed
  The wishes of her soul:
In wild tumultuous bliss, I cry,
  'O Delia, now be kind!'
She pressed me close, and with a sigh,
  To melting joys resigned.

Robert Dodsley 1703-64 · The Progress of Love

Preceding pages: *The Gallant Shepherd – an aristocrat to his soft leather shoes*

January

8

9

10

11

12

13

14

January

15

16

17

18

19

20

21

The Elopement – sweet persuasion of love

January

22

23

24

25

26

27

28

January

_____

29

_____

30

_____

31

_____

Pious Selinda goes to prayers,
    If I but ask the favour;
And yet the tender fool's in tears,
    When she believes I'll leave her.

Would I were free from this restraint,
    Or else had hopes to win her!
Would she could make of me a saint,
    Or I of her a sinner!

William Congreve 1670-1729 · Song

February

_____

1

_____

2

_____

3

_____

4

_____

5

_____

6

_____

7

A circle of dancers in the open air

From books to work, from work to books, I rove,
And am, alas! at leisure to improve! –
Is this the life a beauty ought to lead?
Were eyes so radiant only made to read?
These fingers, at whose touch even age would glow,
Are these of use for nothing but to sew?
Sure erring Nature never could design
To form a housewife in a mould like mine!
O Venus, queen and guardian of the fair,
Attend propitious to thy votary's prayer:
Let me revisit the dear town again:
Let me be seen! – could I that wish obtain,
All other wishes my own power would gain.

Lord George Lyttleton 1709-73
From Soliloquy of a Beauty in the Country

February

8

9

10

11

12

13

14

February

15

16

17

18

19

20

21

February

22

23

24

25

26

27

28/9

March

_____ 1

_____ 2

_____ 3

_____ 4

_____ 5

_____ 6

_____ 7

Dancers and would-be lovers at a ball

Little flowers, little leaves,
Strewn with a light hand,
The young Gods of Spring
Have painted this pretty ribbon.

Take it, West wind, on your wings
And wind it round my sweetheart's dress.
Then she can see herself in the mirror
All in her bright loveliness.

She will see herself wrapped in roses.
As she is young as a rose;
One look at my darling,
And that is reward enough!

Feel what my heart is feeling,
Give me your hand freely,
And our bonds will be stronger
Than this frail ribbon of roses!

Johann Wolfgang von Goethe 1749-1832
A Painted Ribbon

Preceding pages: *The Obliging Shepherd – a bird for his darling*

March

8

9

10

11

12

13

14

March

15

16

17

18

19

20

21

Duet for Two

March

22

23

24

25

26

27

28

March

_____

29

_____

30

_____

31

_____

Never seek to tell thy love
Love that never told can be;
For the gentle wind does move
Silently, invisibly.

I told my love, I told my love,
I told her all my heart,
Trembling, cold, in ghastly fears –
Ah, she doth depart.

William Blake 1757-1827

April

1

2

3

4

5

6

7

Pleading for a kiss?

Here's to the maiden of bashful fifteen!
　　Here's to the widow of fifty!
Here's to the flaunting extravagant quean;
　　And here's to the housewife that's thrifty!
　　　　Let the toast pass,
　　　　Drink to the lass!
　　I'll warrant she'll prove an excuse for the glass!

Here's to the charmer, whose dimples we prize!
　　Now to the maid who has none, sir!
Here's to the girl with a pair of blue eyes;
　　And here's to the nymph with but one, sir!
　　　　Let the toast pass,
　　　　Drink to the lass!
　　I'll warrant she'll prove an excuse for the glass!

Here's to the maid with a bosom of snow!
　　Now to her that's as brown as a berry!
Here's to the wife with a face full of woe,
　　And now to the girl that is merry!
　　　　Let the toast pass,
　　　　Drink to the lass!
　　I'll warrant she'll prove an excuse for the glass!

For let them be clumsy, or let them be slim,
　　Young or ancient, I care not a feather!
So fill a pint bumper, quite up to the brim,
　　And let us e'en toast them together!
　　　　Let the toast pass,
　　　　Drink to the lass!
　　I'll warrant she'll prove an excuse for the glass!

Richard Brinsley Sheridan 1751-1816 · Song

April

8

9

10

11

12

13

14

April

15

16

17

18

19

20

21

International Love – an English sloop engaging a Dutch man-o'-war

455

April

22

23

24

25

26

27

28

April

29

30

The turtle on yon withered bough
    That lately mourned her murdered mate,
Has found another comrade now –
    Such changes, all await!
......
If nature has decreed it so
    With all above, and all below,
Let us like them forget our woe
    And not be killed by sorrow.
If I should quit your arms to-night,
    And chanced to die before 'twas light –
I would advise you – and you might –
    Love again tomorrow.

Philip Freneau 1752-1832 · Song of Thyrsis

May

1

2

3

4

5

6

7

Cherry-picking

As Phyllis the gay, at the break of the day,
    Went forth to the meadows a–maying,
A clown lay asleep by a river so deep,
    That round in meanders was straying.

His bosom was bare, and for whiteness so rare,
    Her heart it was gone without warning,
With cheeks of such hue, that the rose wet with
       dew,
    Ne'er looked half so fresh in a morning.

She culled the new hay, and down by him she lay,
    Her wishes too warm for disguising;
She played with eyes, till he waked in surprise,
    And blushed like the sun at his rising.

She sung him a song, as he leaned on his prong,
    And rested her arm on his shoulder;
She pressed his coy cheek to her bosom so sleek,
    And taught his two arms to enfold her.

The rustic grown kind, by a kiss told his mind,
    And called her his dear and his blessing:
Together they strayed, and sung, frolicked, and
       played,
    And what they did more there's no guessing.

Edward Moore 1712-57 · Song

May

8

9

10

11

12

13

14

May

15

16

17

18

19

20

21

Springtime

May

22

23

24

25

26

27

28

May

29

30

31

Since you went the sun refuses to shine
The sky joins me in weeping for your absence
All our pleasure is gone with you…
Silence reigns everywhere…

Oh come back! Already the shepherds and their
    flocks call for you!
Come back soon, or it will be winter in May.

Jakob Michael Reinhold Lenz 1751-92
From Where Are You?

June

1

2

3

4

5

6

7

The Swing

Oh, my luve's like a red, red rose
   That's newly sprung in June:
O my luve's like the melodie
   That's sweetly play'd in tune.

As fair art thou, my bonie lass,
   So deep in luve am I:
And I will luve thee still, my dear,
   Till a' the seas gang dry.

Till a' the seas gang dry, my dear,
   And the rocks melt wi' the sun;
And I will luve thee still, my dear,
   While the sands o' life shall run.

And fare thee weel, my only luve,
   And fare thee weel a while!
And I will come again, my luve,
   Tho' it were ten thousand mile.

Robert Burns 1759-96 · A Red, Red Rose

June

_____

8

_____

9

_____

10

_____

11

_____

12

_____

13

_____

14

_____

June

15

16

17

18

19

20

21

June

22

23

24

25

26

27

28

June

book, a friend, a song, a glass,
    A chaste, yet laughter-loving lass,
To mortals various joys impart,
    Inform the sense, and warm the heart.

Thrice happy they, who careless, laid,
    Beneath a kind-embowering shade,
With rosy wreaths their temples crown,
    In rosy wine their sorrow drown.
......
Begone ambition, riches, toys,
    And splendid cares, and guilty joys. –
Give me a book, a friend, a glass,
    And a chaste, laughter-loving lass.

William Thompson 1712?-66?
From The Happy Life

In holiday gown, and my new-fangled hat,
    Last Monday I tripped to the fair;
I held up my head, and I'll tell you for what,
    Brisk Roger I guessed would be there:
He woos me to marry whenever we meet,
    There's honey sure dwells on his tongue!
He hugs me so close, and he kisses so sweet,
    I'd wed – if I were not too young.
......
He whispered such soft pretty things in mine ear!
    He flattered, he promised, and swore!
Such trinkets he gave me, such laces and gear,
    That, trust me, – my pockets ran o'er:
Some ballads he bought me, the best he could find,
    And sweetly their burthen he sung;
Good faith! he's so handsome, so witty, and kind,
    I'd wed – if I were not too young.

The sun was just setting, 'twas time to retire,
    (Our cottage was distant a mile)
I rose to be gone – Roger bowed like a squire,
    And handed me over the stile:
His arms he threw round me – love laughed in his eye,
    He led me the meadows among,
There pressed me so close, I agreed, with a sigh,
    To wed – for I was not too young.

John Cunningham 1729-73 · Holiday Gown

Preceding pages: *The Impudent Lover*

July

_____

1

_____

2

_____

3

_____

4

_____

5

_____

6

_____

7

_____

July

8

9

10

11

12

13

14

Love and Victory – Roman style

July

15

16

17

18

19

20

21

When thy beauty appears
In its graces and airs
All bright as an angel new dropp'd from the sky,
At distance I gaze and am awed by my fears:
So strangely you dazzle my eye!

But when without art
Your kind thoughts you impart,
When your love runs in blushes through every
vein;
When it darts from your eyes, when it pants in your
heart,
Then I know you're a woman again.

There is a passion and pride
In our sex (she replied),
And thus, might I gratify both, I would do:
Still an angel appear to each lover beside,
But still be a woman to you.

Thomas Parnell 1679-1718 · Song

July

22

23

24

25

26

27

28

July

_____

29

_____

30

_____

31

_____

The Bolt

August

_____

1

_____

2

_____

3

_____

4

_____

5

_____

6

_____

7

_____

A Gift of Grapes

Had I, Pygmalion like, the power
To make the nymph I would adore;
The model should be thus designed,
Like this her form, like this her mind:
    Her skin should be as lilies fair,
With rosy cheeks and jetty hair:
Her lips with pure vermilion spread,
And soft and moist, as well as red;
......
This for her form: now for her mind;
I'd have it open, generous, kind,
Void of all coquettish arts,
And vain designs of conquering hearts,
Not swayed by any views of gain,
Nor fond of giving others pain;
......
Know all the sciences of love,
Yet ever willing to improve;
To press the hand, and roll the eye,
And drop sometimes an amorous sigh;
To lengthen out the balmy kiss,
And heighten every tender bliss;
And yet I'd have the charmer be
By nature only taught, – or me.

Soame Jenyns 1704-87 · From The Choice

August

8

9

10

11

12

13

14

August

15

16

17

18

19

20

21

Paying the Price of Love – the penitent

August

22

23

24

25

26

27

28

August

_____

29

_____

30

_____

31

_____

"Look upon this rose . . . and this . . ."

September

_____ 1

_____ 2

_____ 3

_____ 4

_____ 5

_____ 6

_____ 7

The Alarm

Oh would the gods but hear my prayer,
To change my form and place me there!
......
I'd never rest till I had found
Which globe was softest, which most round –
Which was most yielding, smooth, and white,
Or the left bosom, or the right;
Which was the warmest, easiest bed,
And which was tipped with purest red.

    Nor could I leave the beauteous scene,
Till I had traced the path between,
That milky way so smooth and even,
That promises to lead to Heav'n:
Lower and lower I'd descend,
To find where it at last would end;
Till fully bless'd I'd wandering rove
O'er all the fragrant Cyprian grove.

    But ah! those wishes all are vain,
The fair one triumphs in my pain...
To flowers that know not to be blessed
The nymph unveils her snowy breast;
While to her slave's desiring eyes
The heavenly prospect she denies:
Too cruel fate, too cruel fair,
To place a senseless nosegay there,
And yet refuse my lips the bliss
To taste one dear transporting kiss.

Soame Jenyns 1704-87
From To a Nosegay in Pancharilla's Breast

September

8

9

10

11

12

13

14

September

15

16

17

18

19

20

21

Titania Wakes – a remarkable love indeed

September

22

23

24

25

26

27

28

September

_____

29

_____

30

_____

False though she be to me and love,
    I'll ne'er pursue revenge;
For still the charmer I approve,
    Though I deplore her change.

In hours of bliss we oft have met,
    They could not always last;
And though the present I regret,
    I'm grateful for the past.

William Congreve 1670-1729 · Song

October

1

2

3

4

5

6

7

The Display of Love's Graces

With the first ring I married youth,
    Grace, Beauty, innocence, and truth;
Taste long admired, sense long revered,
    And all my Molly then appeared.

If she, by merit since disclosed,
    Prove twice the woman I supposed,
I plead that double merit now
    To justify a double vow.

Here then, to-day, with faith as sure,
    With ardour as intense and pure,
As when amidst the rites divine
    I took thy troth, and plighted mine,
To thee, sweet girl, my second ring,
    A token and a pledge I bring;
With this I wed, till death us part,
    Thy riper virtues to my heart…

Samuel Bishop 1731-95 · *From* To His Wife On the Fourteenth
Anniversary of her Wedding-Day, with a ring

October

_____

8

_____

9

_____

10

_____

11

_____

12

_____

13

_____

14

_____

October

15

16

17

18

19

20

21

Brocades and satins among the flowers

October

22

23

24

25

26

27

28

October

29

30

31

When lovely woman stoops to folly,
    And finds too late that men betray,
What charm can soothe her melancholy?
    What art can wash her guilt away?

The only art her guilt to cover,
    To hide her shame from every eye,
To give repentance to her lover,
    And wring his bosom is – to die.

Oliver Goldsmith 1728-74 · *From* The Vicar of Wakefield

November

1

2

3

4

5

6

7

Sweet Daydreams

Of all the girls that are so smart,
　　There's none like pretty Sally;
She is the darling of my heart,
　　And she lives in our alley.
There's ne'er a lady in the land
　　That's half so sweet as Sally;
She is the darling of my heart,
　　And she lives in our alley.

Her father he makes cabbage nets.
　　And thro' the street does cry 'em,
Her mother she sells laces long
　　To such as please to buy 'em.
But sure such folks could ne'er beget
　　So sweet a girl as Sally;
She is the darling of my heart,
　　And she lives in our alley.
......
My master and the neighbours all
　　Make game of me and Sally,
And, but for her, I'd better be
　　A slave and row a galley;
But when my seven long years are out,
　　O then I'll marry Sally,
O then we'll wed, and then we'll bed,
　　But not in our alley.

Henry Carey 1687?-1743
From Sally in our Alley

November

8

9

10

11

12

13

14

November

15

16

17

18

19

20

21

November

22

23

24

25

26

27

28

November

Platonic love! – a pretty name
    For that romantic fire,
When souls confess a mutual flame,
    Devoid of loose desire.

If this new doctrine once prove true,
    I own it something odd is,
That lovers should each other view
    As if they had no bodies.

If spirits thus can live embraced,
    The union may be lasting:
But, faith – 'tis hard the mind should feast,
    And keep its partner fasting.

Samuel Boyse 1708-49   *From* On Platonic Love

December

_____

1

_____

2

_____

3

_____

4

_____

5

_____

6

_____

7

_____

A Winter's Tale

Of all the torments, all the cares
    With which our lives are cursed,
Of all the plagues a lover bears,
    Sure, rivals are the worst!
By partners, in each other kind,
    Afflictions easier grow;
In love alone we hate to find
    Companions of our woe.

Sylvia, for all the pangs you see
    Are labouring in my breast;
I beg not you would favour me,
    Would you but slight the rest!
How great so e'er your rigours are,
    With them alone I'll cope;
I can endure my own despair,
    But not another's hope.

William Walsh 1663-1708 · Rivals in Love

December

8

9

10

11

12

13

14

December

15

16

17

18

19

20

21

December

22

23

24

25

26

27

28

December

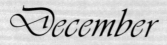

_____

29

_____

30

_____

31

_____

Lamprey's a most immodest diet:
You'll neither wake nor sleep in quiet.
Should I tonight eat sago-cream,
'Twould make me blush to tell my dream:
If I eat lobster, 'tis so warming,
That every man I see looks charming.
......
The shepherdess, who lives on salad,
To cool her youth, controls her palate.

John Gay 1685-1732
From To a Young Lady, with some Lampreys

Epilogue

Having tasted all the pleasures of our separate lives,
let us enjoy the happiness of discovering that none
of them is comparable to that which we once
experienced together, and shall again – to find it
more delicious than before.

Pierre Choderlos de Laclos 1741-1803 · Les Liaisons Dangereuses

After

Picture Credits

Front cover: *Autumn Pastoral,* Francois Boucher, Wallace Collection, London

Half title: *Love and Charity,* Francis Wheatley, Wolverhampton Art Gallery (Ph: Bridgeman)

Title: *L'Amant Supris,* colour engraving after F. J. Schall, British Museum, London (Ph: Bridgeman)

Epilogue: *After,* William Hogarth, Fitzwilliam Museum, Cambridge

Back cover: *Pamela and Mr B. in the Summer House,* Joseph Highmore, Fitzwilliam Museum, Cambridge

Pictures accompanying week starting:

Jan. 1:   *The Fountain,* School of Watteau, Wallace Collection, London

Jan. 21:   *The Story of Laetitia: The Elopement,* George Morland, Christie's, London (Ph: Bridgeman)

Feb. 1:   *La Danse,* Philippe Mercier, Roy Miles Fine Paintings, London (Ph: Bridgeman)

Mar. 1:   *The Costume Ball,* Henri Joseph van Blarengerghe, Musée des Beaux Arts, Lille (Ph: Bridgeman)

Mar. 15: *La Gamme d'Amour,* Antoine Watteau, National Gallery, London (Ph: Bridgeman)

Apri. 1:   *Conversation Galante by a Fountain,* Jean-Baptiste Pater, Wallace Collection, London

Apri. 15: *An English Sloop Engaging a Dutch Man o' War,* Robert Dighton, Whitworth Art Gallery, Manchester

May 1:   *Landscape with Figures Gathering Cherries,* Francois Boucher, Kenwood House, London (Ph: Bridgeman)

May 15:   *Spring,* Johann Georg Platzer (Ph: Picturepoint)

June 1:   *The Swing,* Jean-Honore Fragonard, Wallace Collection, London

June 15: *Pamela and Mr B. in the Summer House,* Joseph Highmore, Fitzwilliam Museum, Cambridge

July 8:   *Rinaldo and Armida,* Giambattista Tiepolo, Private Collection (Ph: Bridgeman)

July 29:   *The Bolt,* Jean-Honore Fragonard, Louvre, Paris (Ph: Bridgeman)

Aug. 1:   *Man Offering Grapes to a Girl,* Francois Boucher, Kenwood House, London (Ph: Bridgeman)

Aug. 15: *The Story of Laetitia: The Fair Penitent,* George Morland, Christie's, London (Ph: Bridgeman)

Aug. 29: *Shepherd and Shepherdess Reposing,* Francois Boucher, Wallace Collection, London

Sept. 1: *The Alarm,* Jean Francois De Troy, Victoria and Albert Museum, London (Ph: Bridgeman)

Sept. 15: *Le Reveil de Titania,* Henry Fuseli, Kunsthaus, Zurich (Ph: Bridgeman)

Oct. 1: *A Rustic Party,* Nicolas Lancret, Private Collection (Ph: Bridgeman)

Oct. 15: *Relaxation in the Country,* Jean-Baptiste Pater, Musée des Beaux-Arts, Valenciennes (Ph: Bridgeman)

Nov. 1: *The Souvenir,* Jean Honore Fragonard, Wallace Collection, London

Nov. 15: *Concert Champètre,* Jean-Baptiste Pater, Musée des Beaux-Arts, Valenciennes (Ph: Bridgeman)

Dec. 1: *Lacing her Skates,* Nicolas Lancret, Private Collection (Ph: Bridgeman)

Dec. 15: *Before,* William Hogarth, Fitzwilliam Museum, Cambridge

Double page pictures following week ending:

Jan. 7: *The Gallant Shepherd,* Francois Boucher, Hotel de Soubise, Paris (Ph: Bridgeman)

Mar. 7: *The Obliging Shepherd,* Francois Boucher, Hotel de Soubise, Paris (Ph: Bridgeman)

June 30: *A Feast,* Nicolas Lancret, Private Collection (Ph: Bridgeman)

**Picture frames supplied by kind permission of
Paul Mitchell Ltd., 99 New Bond Street, London**